THE WHALES OF AUGUST

A PLAY IN TWO ACTS BY
DAVID BERRY

★

DRAMATISTS
PLAY SERVICE
INC.

THE WHALES OF AUGUST was first presented as a staged reading as part of Center Stage First Stage Series, Baltimore, Maryland, on April 8, 1980. It was directed by Bill Ludel; the scenery was by Hugh Landwehr; the costumes were by Lesley Skannal; the lighting was by Bonnie Ann Brown; and the sound was by David Campbell. The cast, in order of appearance, was as follows:

LIBBY . . . . Kate Wilkinson
SARAH . . . . Margaret Thomson
TISHA . . . . Vivienne Shub
MARANOV . . . . Louis Beachner

THE WHALES OF AUGUST was presented by Trinity Square Repertory Co. at the Lederer Theatre, Providence, Rhode Island, on February 17, 1981. It was directed by Adrian Hall; the scenery was by Robert D. Soule; the costumes were by William Lane; and the lighting was by John F. Custer. The cast, in order of appearance, was as follows:

SARAH . . . . Sylvia Davis
LIBBY . . . . Ruth Maynard
JOSHUA . . . . Hilmar Sallee
TISHA . . . . Vivienne Shub
MARANOV . . . . Daniel Nagrin

THE WHALES OF AUGUST was presented in New York City by the WPA Theatre (Kyle Renick, Producing Director) in February, 1982. It was directed by William Ludel; the setting was by Edward T. Gianfrancesco; costumes were by David Murin; and the lighting was by Phil Monat. The cast, in order of appearance, was as follows:

SARAH . . . . Bettie Endrizzi
LIBBY . . . . Elizabeth Council
TISHA . . . . Vivienne Shub
JOSHUA . . . . Daniel Keyes
MARANOV . . . . George Lloyd

CAST OF CHARACTERS

SARAH: Sarah Louise Logan Webber, 75 years of age.
LIBBY: Elizabeth Mae Logan Strong, 86 years of age.
JOSHUA: Joshua Brackett, 80 years of age.
TISHA: Letitia Benson Doughty, 78 years of age.
MARANOV: Nicholas Maranov, 79 years of age.

PLACE: An island on the Maine coast.

TIME: An August weekend, 1954.

DEDICATION

For my grandfather, William Finlay Adams
23 June 1886 - 20 March 1977

ACKNOWLEDGEMENT

I wish to express my thanks to the National Endowment for the Arts, whose 1978 Creative Writing Fellowship supported in part the creation of this play.

—DAB—

AUTHOR'S NOTES

The struggle to affirm and to enhance life continues throughout a life. Difficult choices are not diminished in degree even into the antechamber of death. In Samuel Beckett's phrase, the characters of this play "keep on keeping on." For these characters, old age is a fact—not a negative state. The future to which Joshua Brackett refers (and which he says he doesn't like) is our present; but, in the present tense of the play, "senior citizen" hasn't entered the vocabulary nor has old age been yet relegated to a second-class condition.

In this spirit, clichés and caricatures of old people must be avoided in playing these roles, just as the play itself avoids them. These minds are not slow; these bodies are not infirm beyond the normal lessening of physical strength in old age. These people are trying to choose *how to live*, not to die. In that spirit of life-affirmation, Sarah's final choice is the key: one *can* choose to do something radically new and bold, even when, statistically and chronologically, one's day might be one's very last turn on the mortal coil.

A *caveat*: pay close attention to the indicated pauses. If "long pause" is indicated, observe it, fill it, let us see the thinking process of the character. The rhythm of the play is crisp except where indicated by pauses. This is particularly true in the play's last scene when the play can be felt to end too abruptly if the richness of life and choice and struggle within the pauses is not fully played or allowed by direction.

David Berry
Wakefield, Rhode Island
March 1984

DESCRIPTION OF STAGE SETTING

The play's action takes place in a single setting with two major playing areas: the living room interior and the wrap-around exterior porch of Sarah's summer cottage, perched on ledges above an ocean sound with a nor' east exposure to the open Atlantic Ocean.

Across the Upstage wall from Right to Left are the following principal features of the living room:

1) A doorway entrance to the living room from the unseen (or partially seen) kitchen in the Up Right corner.
2) Just Left of the kitchen door (or seen just inside the kitchen) is a large closet used for household maintenance items.
3) Left of the closet is Libby's space, defined by a standard two-over-two window (through which can be seen ledges and spruce tree branches) in front of which are placed Libby's platform rocker, an adjoining side table with Zenith tabletop radio, and footstool.
4) Left of Libby's territory and nearly centered on the Upstage wall is a large, soot-and-heat stained natural brick fireplace. On its mantel are at least the following items: one silver candlestick, boxed wooden matches, and a photograph, sepia-toned with age, of Sarah's deceased husband Philip, wearing a World War I Army lieutenant's uniform and cap.
5) Left of the fireplace is the bathroom door, opening into the Upstage wall, through which when opened can be seen a bathtub on clawed feet.

Moving from Upstage Left downstage are the following principal features of the living room:

1) Sarah's bedroom door, leading Off Left.
2) Downstage of Sarah's door are a lid top desk and companion chair, above which is a 40's vintage wall telephone unit.
3) Just Downstage of the desk is Libby's bedroom door, also leading Off Left.

Downstage of the fireplace, nearly centered in the room, is a cluster arrangement of furniture (social space) including a wicker settee, a side table with lamp, a captain's chair, and another occasional chair (possibly a rocker). The side table in this cluster must be sufficiently large enough and lightweight enough to accommodate Sarah's use of it as her "anniversary" table.

Moving Downstage from Up Right corner are the following principal features of the living room:

1) This Right wall of the living room faces toward the open sea. Centered in the wall are two standard two-over-two windows, which are the windows to be replaced by the "new picture window" mentioned in the text. These windows, however represented in design, define the dining area of the cottage: a table large enough to accommodate four matching chairs over which is suspended a Tiffany-style hanging lamp.
2) Downstage of the dining area is an old, low, game chest on which are placed a stereopticon with cards and 30's editions of jigsaw puzzles, Parcheesi, Chinese Checkers, Monopoly, and Mah-Jonng.

It is necessary to have an entrance to the living room from the porch. Depending upon space limitations and sight lines, that door (represented by a working screened door) should be placed on the living room's Right exterior wall—either Upstage of the dining area, or Downstage of it at the living room's Down Right corner. If placed Downstage, the door should open out onto the porch where it will provide a useful, dramatically vivid space: a landing with two steps leading up to entrance. In fact, it is useful to define a separation from living room and porch by raising the living room from porch level.

The porch space needs the following items of furniture: three rough-hewn rocking chairs with simple cushions over rushed seats; a small side table which is used alternately as a space for tea/coffee service and as a place for Sarah to rest Libby's hairdressing items. Also, the porch should have an Upstage Right boardwalk entrance.

NOTES ON SET DRESSING AND STYLE AND COLOURS

The interior reflects rather typical turn-of-the—century Maine cottage construction—far more modest than the "cottages" of Watch Hill or Bar Harbor design. The walls are simple tongued-and-grooved vertical boards in their natural wood colours. The floor is hardwood and painted in neutral colour. All interior window and door casings are also natural wood. The window behind Libby's space can have an old-fashioned green roller shade and simple box curtains.

As much furniture as can be effectively placed in this interior is desirable, since such artifacts lend weight and substance to a past which gives the room a special ambience. Victorian, Twenties, and Thirties pieces mix harmoniously with rough-hewn local items; hooked or braided rugs are mixed with scattered Oriental rugs; wherever possible, the walls hold American Indian baskets, framed embroidered homilies, amateur seascapes, old photos of "homey hearth" scenes, and knick-knack shelves. Table surfaces and shelves yield a lifetime's random collection: odds and ends of carnival glass, milk glass, cut glass; brass vases with dried flowers, exotic sea shells, Oriental and European china or vases; old books; the likes of an ostrich egg on a teak stand, etc. Additionally, a couple of items should be prominently visible which indicate the particular time of the play: perhaps a photo of President Eisenhower or General MacArthur-in-Korea, or an item or two of furniture representing early Fifties style.

The porch floor is painted a sand-beige. If exterior walls are represented, they are faced with cedar shingles naturally weathered to a soft silver-grey. Exterior window casings and door casings are painted a pale blue. Any suggestion of porch railings should be simple rather than ornate and should never resemble anything which would suggest a "beach" cottage. Whatever can be done to suggest both proximity to the sea and a cottage placed high on rocky ledges above the sea is desirable.

THE WHALES OF AUGUST

ACT I

Scene 1

As the scene opens, the bright golden early morning light of a cloudless August day floods the living room and porch from R. and front. Reflections from the rippling ocean sound dapple the set D., diminishing as the scene progresses and the sun climbs higher. In the opening silence, gentle waves wash the rocks below, a bell buoy sounds intermittently, and the clamour of gulls is heard nearby.

Sarah enters U.R. on the porch boardwalk singing snatches of "Pack Up Your Troubles In Your Old Kit Bag." Her movements betray a strong femininity, warming grace, and, at the same time, a quality of Yankee competence and strength. She wears a rather shapeless dress, beige and with buttons all down the front, sturdy hose, stodgy black lace-up shoes, and a hair net which doesn't quite contain all of her softly-waved grey hair. She carries a wicker laundry basket which she sets on a porch rocker. She withdraws from the basket a red rose and a white rose which she sniffs briefly, then carefully lays the roses back in the basket and removes several dish towels to hang over the porch rail to dry. When she finishes hanging the towels, she straightens, looks at the sea for the first time, and takes a deep breath.

SARAH. Not a cloud, not one. (*Peering intently forward and down.*) Is that a seal? I think it is! (*Pause.*) No . . . just a log. (*Looks seaward again, and follows the flight of a single gull as it cries and flies from R. to L.*) The herring are running! (*Movement on the rocks below catches her eye, withdraws hanky from bosom and waves.*) Yoo-hoo! Mr. Maranov! Yoo-hoo! (*Pause.*) Can't hear you! Hope you catch something! (*Final wave, replaces hanky, enters living room with basket.*) Libby, it's a beautiful morning. You should take some sun. (*Puts basket away in kitchen U.R., returns to living room with dust cloth.*) Where does it all come from? (*Starts about the room with a determined brushing of the dust-catchers.*) Gracious . . . look at that brass . . . (*Pauses at mantel photograph, dusts it gently and blows a kiss to it.*) Forty-two years, Philip. Just think. (*Libby's bedroom door opens and she enters. She is handsome and possesses an imperious dignity. She wears a mauve dress much in the same design as Sarah's dress, but its buttons are unevenly fastened near the bottom so that one panel is hitched up. She wears heavy support hose and an old pair of slippers. Her hair is a long mane, rather unkempt, very white and luxurious. She wears no glasses.*)

LIBBY. Is someone here?

SARAH. No, dear. Just talking to myself.

LIBBY. Anybody answer?

SARAH. Not today.

LIBBY. (*Making slow and careful way to her platform rocker.*) Wouldn't we be surprised if someone did?

SARAH. We certainly would. (*Notices breakfast tray on Libby's side table.*) Libby, you didn't eat a speck of your breakfast again.

LIBBY. I don't want it.

SARAH. Your tea must be cold.

LIBBY. Yes.

SARAH. Your cereal, too.

LIBBY. Logical.

SARAH. Libby, you haven't eaten breakfast all week.

LIBBY. I don't need it.

SARAH. It's the most important meal of the day.

LIBBY. (*Sitting.*) I'm not hungry, not hungry at all.

SARAH. You shouldn't do without breakfast.

LIBBY. This is the mauve dress, isn't it?

SARAH. (*Looks, notices the uneven buttoning, goes to Libby to re-button her dress.*) You're not wearing your shoes.

LIBBY. I couldn't find them.

SARAH. Perhaps you kicked them under your bed.

LIBBY. I don't know.

SARAH. You really should eat something.

LIBBY. Mauve was always a favorite colour of mine.

SARAH. (*Finished re-buttoning, rises.*) I'll get your shoes for you.

LIBBY. You didn't answer me.

SARAH. Answer what, dear?

LIBBY. I asked if this were the mauve dress.

SARAH. Oh. Yes, dear, it is. (*Resumes dusting.*)

LIBBY. I didn't forget that I asked.

SARAH. No, dear.

LIBBY. I don't forget things, y' know.

SARAH. No, dear.

LIBBY. What are you doing?

SARAH. Dusting.

LIBBY. You dusted yesterday.

SARAH. I did?

LIBBY. Yes.

SARAH. Well . . . I can't keep up with it.

LIBBY. Busy, busy, busy . . .

SARAH. I've simply given up on the brass.

LIBBY. I always liked it better tarnished.

SARAH. It's the ocean dampness . . .

LIBBY. I'm glad the silver's stored away. You'd be at *that* all the time.

SARAH. Oh Libby . . .

13

LIBBY. Are your duties finished for the Fair?

SARAH. I've hardly made a dent in them.

LIBBY. You're usually finished in July.

SARAH. I know, but with one thing and another, I just can't keep up. (*Pause.*) The summer's going so quickly.

LIBBY. I wish we were back home in Philadelphia.

SARAH. Libby, it's so hot in Philadelphia now!

LIBBY. I like the heat. *You* can't be busy in it.

SARAH. I've almost finished with the aprons I'm making for the Fancy Goods Table. (*Pauses in her dusting.*) And I've collected some things for the White Elephant Table . . . and . . . what else . . . ?

LIBBY. Potholders? Those knitted things?

SARAH. Not this year.

LIBBY. Argyle socks?

SARAH. Last year, Libby. I do them only on the odd numbered years.

LIBBY. Salt water taffy for the Candy Table?

SARAH. No . . . (*Pause.*) I am donating that old stereopticon to the Silent Auction Table. They say they're quite valuable nowadays.

LIBBY. We'd be pretty valuable, too, if we were stereopticons.

SARAH. I should think so. A matched pair.

LIBBY. My, my . . . what would the Annual Fair *be* without Sarah Webber?

SARAH. It's a worthy cause, dear. (*Resumes dusting.*)

LIBBY. The world is full of worthy causes.

SARAH. Yes, indeed.

LIBBY. And you're always in line for most of 'em.

SARAH. I was trained to do for others.

LIBBY. Well . . . Mr. Barnum said there was one born every minute.

SARAH. (*Pause.*) I did promise to make something else for the Fair . . .

LIBBY. Plans.

SARAH. No. (*Pause.*) What did you say?

LIBBY. I said, "plans." (*Brief pause, then quickly.*) Remember your plans for the Grand Tour? You never got past Cousin Minnie's house in Belfast, though.

SARAH. No, I didn't.

LIBBY. Barnum's maxim again, Sarah.

SARAH. Now Libby, Aunt Mary was very ill.

LIBBY. Yes. And, besides, "doing for others is a way of doing for one's self." (*Sarcastically.*)

SARAH. Libby, I did see quite a bit of Ulster. County Down, County Antrim, the Giant's Causeway. (*Pauses in her dusting to turn briefly to Libby.*) I even bowled on the green in Bangor — *twice.* (*Resumes dusting.*)

LIBBY. (*After a pause.*) November is a time for departures, you know.

SARAH. Hmm?

LIBBY. August isn't bad as a choice, but November is more appropriate.

SARAH. (*Exiting to kitchen.*) Well, thank goodness it isn't November!

LIBBY. Ishmael joined Captain Ahab's crew when it was November in his soul.

SARAH. (*Off.*) Who, dear?

LIBBY. Ishmael, Sarah! In Mr. Melville's book!

SARAH. (*Off.*) Oh . . .

LIBBY. *Moby Dick.* Didn't you ever read *Moby Dick*?!

SARAH. (*Enters carrying a tall white taper for the mantel candlestick.*) You were always the reader in the family, dear, but I know the book you mean . . . the one about the white whale. (*Places taper in candlestick.*)

LIBBY. That's the one.

SARAH. (*Brief pause at mantel.*) Stuffed animals! *That's* what I forgot! For the Toy Table. Right after the aprons. (*Resumes dusting.*)

LIBBY. (*After a pause.*) You sailed for Belfast in November. November, nineteen and ten.

15

SARAH. I believe I did.

LIBBY. Yes, and you considered returning on the Titanic.

SARAH. It's a good thing I didn't!

LIBBY. Oh, I don't know. If you'd survived, you'd have had a lot to talk about for the rest of your life.

SARAH. Indeed. But, I came back on the Olympic instead, without incident.

LIBBY. Shipwreck would have been so thrilling.

SARAH. I'm not cut out for that sort of thrill.

LIBBY. Is that so?

SARAH. Yes. (*Pauses in her chore D.C.*) You know, I believe we'll see the whales this weekend.

LIBBY. Now *that* would be a surprise.

SARAH. It's time for them.

LIBBY. They don't come anymore.

SARAH. They were here last summer.

LIBBY. Right out here, in the sound?

SARAH. Of course.

LIBBY. I didn't hear them.

SARAH. (*A slight pause.*) Well, they were too far offshore.

LIBBY. I see.

SARAH. Besides, the herring are running. That's a sure sign.

LIBBY. Signs fail, y' know.

SARAH. Libby Strong, I shall see them and you will hear them, right out front, just as we always have! (*She exits into kitchen with dust cloth.*)

LIBBY. (*Pause.*) When you were a little girl, Sarah, you thought the whales made the seasons change.

SARAH. (*Re-entering and pausing in her cross.*) I did?

LIBBY. Yes. You told Father that the whales caught the wind with their tails and hauled it down from the Arctic.

SARAH. I *do* remember that.

LIBBY. Tisha'a coming, isn't she?

SARAH. Yes, dear.

LIBBY. Then I should have my shoes.

SARAH. Of course, dear. (*Crosses to exit into Libby's room.*)
With all this reminiscing, I forgot.

LIBBY. I want to look presentable.

SARAH. (*Off.*) What did you do with them?

LIBBY. I didn't do anything.

SARAH. (*Off.*) Did you look for them?

LIBBY. Yes, Sarah!

SARAH. (*Off.*) I found them. (*Enters with shoes.*) You must
have kicked them under the bureau. (*Gives shoes to Libby.*)

LIBBY. (*Starts putting on shoes, hands slippers to Sarah.*)
You needn't hover, Sarah.

SARAH. (*Doing just that, she retreats a small distance to
observe Libby's efforts.*) Of course not, dear.

LIBBY. (*After her shoes are on.*) Will you have time to brush
my hair?

SARAH. I do have some more tidying to do.

LIBBY. Oh, if it's *such* a bother . . .

SARAH. No, dear, no bother. (*Exits to Libby's room with
slippers.*)

LIBBY. Perhaps outside would be nice.

SARAH. (*Off.*) Yes, there's no breeze.

LIBBY. (*Rises, crosses slowly to porch.*) Will you bring my
brooch, too?

SARAH. (*Off.*) Yes, dear. (*Libby makes her way outside
through the screened door, takes a deep breath once on porch
landing, then crosses D. to her porch rocker. Sarah enters
from bedroom, follows to porch with brush, comb, hairpins
and brooch.*)

LIBBY. (*Sitting in rocker.*) Do make me look presentable.

SARAH. You always look presentable. (*Arranges items on
side table, and takes her place behind Libby after placing
brooch in Libby's hand.*)

LIBBY. I expect I'm a great bother to you.

SARAH. Nothing of the sort. (*Pause; Sarah begins the
brushing.*) Mr. Maranov is fishing on our rocks.

LIBBY. I hope he doesn't offer his catch to us.

17

SARAH. He usually gets a fine bunch of cunners.

LIBBY. I will not eat any of those fish!

SARAH. Oh, for heaven's sake—

LIBBY. Sewer fish—that's what they are.

SARAH. Nonsense. The currents are very strong.

LIBBY. I will not eat anything caught off these rocks.

SARAH. The fish are perfectly delicious.

LIBBY. They are disgusting! Our sewage goes right out that ugly pipe.

SARAH. Do you think that I would eat them if I were worried?

LIBBY. You'd do anything to flatter that fraud.

SARAH. He's *not* a fraud.

LIBBY. *Baron* Maranov, indeed.

SARAH. Helen Parsons has seen photographs of him and his mother at the Tsar's court.

LIBBY. That was so long ago it could be anybody.

SARAH. According to Helen, the resemblance is unmistakable.

LIBBY. I will not eat his fish.

SARAH. You don't have to!

LIBBY. There, you see. I *am* a bother.

SARAH. You're just being silly about those fish.

LIBBY. You're not much for complaining, but I can feel it from you.

SARAH. I remind you, Elizabeth Mae, that I was the one who volunteered to move into your house in Germantown after your operations.

LIBBY. You had just lost your Philip.

SARAH. Yes.

LIBBY. Well, I suppose you could change your mind.

SARAH. Whatever for?

LIBBY. I do have my Anna.

SARAH. Your Anna has never wanted to be involved in our lives.

LIBBY. She *is* my daughter.

SARAH. Only at Christmas, it would seem.

LIBBY. I know what you're thinking.

SARAH. Yes, and we've had this very same discussion since the Depression. She's never been very daughterly and you've never been very motherly, and that's *that*. Now, hold still while I get out this snarl.

LIBBY. Ouch! (*Pause.*) Do you remember the swans in the park when we were children?

SARAH. Yes.

LIBBY. Mother had hair like that. I suppose you wouldn't remember.

SARAH. No.

LIBBY. Is my hair as white as the swans?

SARAH. I expect it is.

LIBBY. You're not fibbing?

SARAH. Why should I?

LIBBY. Not yellowing at all?

SARAH. No, dear.

LIBBY. I've always had beautiful hair.

SARAH. Um-hmn.

LIBBY. Matthew thought it was my crowning glory.

SARAH. Matthew was right.

LIBBY. What colour is your hair now?

SARAH. Grey. The brown's all gone.

LIBBY. Nothing's forever.

SARAH. So you always say.

LIBBY. I do?

SARAH. Several times a week.

LIBBY. Some things bear repeating.

SARAH. I suppose.

LIBBY. Many times.

SARAH. I hear them.

LIBBY. I don't think so.

SARAH. Hold still, dear.

LIBBY. (*Pause.*) Quite white you say?

SARAH. What?

19

LIBBY. My hair.

SARAH. Oh, yes . . . quite.

LIBBY. (*Pause.*) Matthew and I used to sit in the park. (*Pause.*) Parks are for children, and lovers in springtime.

SARAH. Ah . . . yes . . .

LIBBY. I haven't been to a park for a long time.

SARAH. Being here is like being in a park.

LIBBY. No swans, though. (*Pause.*) Swans mate for life, you know.

SARAH. Is that a fact?

LIBBY. Yes. (*Pause.*) Did you and Philip think it was for life?

SARAH. Why . . . yes.

LIBBY. Life fooled you.

SARAH. Yes, it did.

LIBBY. Always does.

SARAH. (*Pause.*) Tomorrow is Philip's and my forty-second anniversary.

LIBBY. Last Valentine's Day, it was sixty-six years for Matthew and me.

SARAH. Gracious . . .

LIBBY. Yes . . . you were only nine when I married him.

SARAH. Wasn't I a good flower girl?

LIBBY. You stepped on my train. (*Pause.*) Matthew died in November.

SARAH. So he did. November, nineteen and . . .

LIBBY. Thirty-four.

SARAH. Has it really been twenty years?

LIBBY. Yes. I was sixty-six when he died. (*Pause.*) When did the four of us take that trip out West?

SARAH. Right after the War, dear. Not too long after Philip came home from France.

LIBBY. Yes . . . you two were always creeping away to be alone.

SARAH. It *was* our anniversary.

LIBBY. It wasn't an important one.

SARAH. It was to *me*.

LIBBY. (*Slight pause.*) Wasn't it nice of Teddy Roosevelt to put those National Parks all over the place?

SARAH. Very thoughtful of him.

LIBBY. Trouble is, they're always in the middle of nowhere. He didn't put any of 'em close to home. (*Pause.*) It would be lovely to sit in a park for a while. It's such a nice day for November.

SARAH. (*Halts brushing.*) Libby . . .

LIBBY. I know what month this is! This August I know.

SARAH. (*Resumes brushing.*) Good, dear.

LIBBY. I don't forget things.

SARAH. I think you forgot your breakfast.

LIBBY. That was a *choice*.

SARAH. All right, dear. (*Finishes brushing, starts combing.*)

LIBBY. I had such trouble taking care of your hair. A little ragamuffin you were.

SARAH. A bit of a tomboy, I guess.

LIBBY. Always creeping about and hiding in trees.

SARAH. No more trees for me.

LIBBY. Why not?

SARAH. I creak too much around the edges. (*Stops combing, begins wrapping Libby's hair in an elegant, simple twist.*)

LIBBY. Just close your eyes and climb a tree.

SARAH. Haven't got time. (*In silence, places hairpins in Libby's coif.*) There, there, there. All done.

LIBBY. Do you know why old ladies sit on park benches, Sarah?

SARAH. Why, dear?

LIBBY. To hold them for springtime lovers. Even the benches want to get away in November.

SARAH. Libby, this is August.

LIBBY. Whatever you wish, Sarah. The time doesn't matter.

SARAH. Of course it does.

LIBBY. Only if you wear it like a wet blanket.

SARAH. (*Gathering up hair things.*) Are you going to stay outside a while?

LIBBY. Yes, Sarah.

SARAH. All right, dear. (*Starts to exit with hair things.*)

LIBBY. Bring me that hat from Albuquerque.

SARAH. I'll get it for you, dear. (*Enters living room to retrieve outsized "tourist" sombrero.*)

LIBBY. (*While Sara is inside.*) You think I forget the time, but I don't. All the time is mine. It's what's left to me.

SARAH. (*Enters porch, pauses.*) Are you sure you want to stay outside, dear?

LIBBY. Yes. Go about your chores, Sarah. I'll hold the bench. (*Puts on sombrero.*)

SARAH. Your favorite programs are coming on. It's almost time for Arthur Godfrey and Break the Bank.

LIBBY. I don't need the radio anymore. (*She shivers slightly.*)

SARAH. Are you all right, dear?

LIBBY. He's so close, Sarah. My bones are in his November reach.

SARAH. (*Pause.*) Whose reach, Libby?

LIBBY. The escort. Not so very far away, the door will open and in he'll come, wearing an old bathrobe soiled with the residues of all the times, the stains and streaks and smears . . . and tears . . . tears from a thousand eyes.

SARAH. Libby!

LIBBY. A time for departure, damp and drizzly — November, you see! Matthew's month will be mine!

SARAH. Elizabeth Mae, I won't listen to this!

LIBBY. Hush, child. You must!

SARAH. No! We don't have much time left, Libby. I'd like the last of it to be pleasant!

LIBBY. Then stop making plans!! (*Sarah exits into living room.*)

MODERATE FADE TO BLACK

ACT 1

Scene 2

Later the same morning; the sun is climbing toward its noon peak, leaving the porch brightly illuminated and the living room in greater shade.

Libby remains on the porch, drowzing in the day's warmth. Sarah sits at the dining table, surrounded by her apron project materials. Her attention to the task at hand shifts to Libby, whom she can see out a window; and we see her lost in thought in mid-stitch.

TISHA. (*Off.*) Hal-loo-oo! Hello! Hello! Hello!
SARAH. Coming! (*Entering in a burst from the kitchen, Tisha is a pert woman, rather like a cross between a bantam rooster and an animated feather duster. She fans herself with a straw hat which has brims like a manta ray's wings; her dress and its colorations may seem a bit youthful for her age but she carries her style with élan and no self-consciousness.*)
TISHA. Let m'self in, dear. Thought you might be off in a corner. (*She has a pronounced Maine accent.*)
SARAH. (*Meeting Tisha in a warm embrace.*) Hello, dear.
TISHA. Sara . . . brought you these blackberries I picked. (*Hands small pail to Sarah.*)
SARAH. Thank you, Tisha.
TISHA. Phewl! Got m'self a bit warm walkin' down here.
SARAH. You walked?

23

TISHA. I did.

SARAH. Is something wrong with your car?

TISHA. No, but let's not talk about that. (*Pause.*) You look peaked, dear. Anything the matter?

SARAH. No, dear.

TISHA. I see. What's that cantankerous sister of yours done now?

SARAH. Nothing.

TISHA. Well then . . . a touch of the collywobbles? (*Pause.*) Nope. It's Libby for sure.

SARAH. You know me too well.

TISHA. Ayuh. Fifty years of crossin' bridges together will do that. Now, out with it.

SARAH. She didn't eat breakfast again. It's the fourth time this week.

TISHA. So?

SARAH. Tisha, she has always eaten breakfast, every day of her life. (*Sees breakfast tray on Libby's table.*) Oh, I haven't put away her tray.

TISHA. You needn't be tidy on my account, Sarah Webber.

SARAH. I should have done it hours ago.

TISHA. Oh, piffle! C'mon, what else has Libby done?

SARAH. (*Pause.*) She's started talking about dying.

TISHA. She has?

SARAH. Yes. She says she'll go in November, like Matthew. She says death is waiting for her now.

TISHA. Sarah, that woman's as healthy as a horse.

SARAH. I know it. (*Pause.*) I think it's her mind.

TISHA. Failin', is it?

SARAH. I could be wrong. I might be imagining things.

TISHA. Oh, foot, Sarah Webber. You were a nurse. You know what's happenin', dear. (*Pause, then quietly.*) Where is she?

SARAH. Out on the porch.

TISHA. (*Going to Sarah.*) Good. We can have a heart-to-heart then. (*Draws Sarah to seating cluster below fireplace.*)

24

Now, sit down. (*Sarah sits and Tisha follows suit.*) What're you gonna do about it?

SARAH. What can I do?

TISHA. Sarah, Libby was a difficult woman in the best of times.

SARAH. Oh yes, it's never been easy.

TISHA. You've done your duty.

SARAH. Have I?

TISHA. Yes, you have. Fifteen years, dear, is world enough and time for all your real and imagined debts to be cleared even. (*Pause.*) What about Anna? Have you told her?

SARAH. No, no one but you.

TISHA. I think you should ask her to take Libby.

SARAH. Tisha!

TISHA. Ayuh.

SARAH. Anna wouldn't keep her. She'd place Libby somewhere.

TISHA. Anna's got plenty of money. She'll see to it that her mother's well cared for.

SARAH. How'd you like to be shuffled about like that?

TISHA. Well, Sarah, you know what Mr. Truman said.

SARAH. What?

TISHA. If the buck is passed, it might as well be passed to somebody with piles of 'em.

TISHA. He didn't say that!

TISHA. 'Course he didn't. But you get my drift. Anna's where it stops, Sarah, not with you.

SARAH. I'd die of shame if I put Libby away.

TISHA. You'll die of overwork if y' keep her. (*Pause.*) Sara . . . if y' did it, would you be able to manage?

SARAH. What do you mean, Tisha?

TISHA. (*Pause.*) Money, dear.

SARAH. Well, I suppose the Philadelphia house might be sold . . . but that belongs to Libby.

TISHA. What about this place, dear? Could you keep it?

SARAH. I think I could . . . get by, Tisha.

25

TISHA. How about the winters, Sarah? You'd have to get a place to stay, somewhere. That'd be a heap of money you aren't used to findin'.

SARAH. I hadn't really thought that far . . .

TISHA. Got to, dear. And I have an answer. (*Pause.*) You could come stay with me.

SARAH. Oh, Tisha . . . thank you. But I wouldn't want to burden you with my troubles.

TISHA. Oh, half o' life is troubles, dear, and the other half is gettin' over 'em. You come stay with me, and we'll get through it together. (*Pause.*) Besides, I think it's time you retired your nursin' pin.

SARAH. What else do I know?

TISHA. You could learn to practice on yourself, dear. (*There is suddenly a great clangor from underneath the cottage, as of a wrench striking pipes.*)

SARAH. (*Rising and crossing U. to bathroom corner where she addresses the floor.*) What are you doing?!

JOSHUA. (*From below; he speaks with a pronounced Down East accent.*) I'm turnin' your water off! (*Another clank.*)

LIBBY. (*On porch.*) Sarah! What's happening?

SARAH. Oh, Lord . . . (*Crosses close enough to porch door to call out to Libby.*) It's Joshua, Libby.

LIBBY. Can't you tell him to be quieter?

SARAH. I've tried for fifty years, dear. (*Crosses back to bathroom corner.*) Joshua! It's the bathroom *faucets* that leak!

JOSHUA. (*Below.*) If I don't cut the main, you'll be gettin' a damn sight more'n leaks!

SARAH. The kettle's on! Why don't you come up for a cup of tea before you begin?

JOSHUA. (*Below.*) Jesus Lord above . . . takes me half the day to get in here and the other half to get out . . .

SARAH. (*Crossing to kitchen.*) I've waited for you since June, Joshua! (*To Tisha.*) I guess I can wait another few minutes. Will you have some tea, Tisha?

TISHA. Ayuh, thank you, dear.

JOSHUA. (*Below.*) This goddamned crawl space ain't got any bigger since I was here last . . .

LIBBY. Joshua Brackett, stop your swearing!

SARAH. (*Off, in kitchen, as off-stage back door slams.*) Hello, Joshua.

JOSHUA. (*Off.*) Mornin', Mrs. Webber. How be ya?

SARAH. I'm fine, Joshua, but I think you'd better go make peace with my sister.

JOSHUA. (*Off.*) If I must, I must. (*Joshua enters living room from kitchen. He is a robust man with a ruddy complexion. He wears coveralls, freshly smudged with rust and dirt from below; his shirt is very faded flannel, and he wears heavy workboots and sports a railroad cap from which tufts of white hair escape around the sides. He carries an old wooden tool box, which he drops on the floor with a loud thud.*) Well, hello, Mrs. Doughty.

TISHA. Good mornin', Joshua.

LIBBY. Is that you, Tisha?

TISHA. (*Calling out to porch.*) Mornin', Libby! (*Rising.*) I guess we both better pay our respects.

JOSHUA. Ayuh . . . (*Tisha and Joshua exit to porch.*) How do, Mrs. Strong?

LIBBY. Better if you'd keep down the clatter, Mr. Brackett.

JOSHUA. I'll do m' best, Mrs. Strong, I'll do m' very best.

TISHA. Libby, will you join us for some tea?

LIBBY. I believe I'll wait for Mr. Brackett to finish his chores.

TISHA. All right, dear. (*Tisha and Joshua re-enter living room, and Joshua pauses in doorway, looks at Libby, and deliberately allows the screen door to slam behind him.*) Joshua, you are incorrigible.

JOSHUA. Ayuh . . . that, too. (*Crossing to Tisha who has taken her seat.*) How be ya, Mrs. Doughty?

TISHA. (*In imitation of Libby.*) "Better if you'd keep down the clatter, Mr. Brackett."

JOSHUA. Ayuh . . . she's a corker, that one.

TISHA. Ayuh . . . a right wicked caution.

SARAH. (*Entering with tea tray.*) Have a seat, Joshua.

JOSHUA. (*Doffs cap, sits in captain's chair.*) Thank you, Mrs. Webber.

SARAH. (*Pouring tea.*) Well, I haven't seen you since you turned the water on. How've you been?

JOSHUA. I been fine.

TISHA. Been keepin' busy, Joshua?

JOSHUA. The usual, Mrs. Doughty.

TISHA. I expect so. Lot o' newcomers on the island.

JOSHUA. Ayuh . . . too damned many if y' ask me.

SARAH. They do bring you business, Joshua.

JOSHUA. Nope. The Winter does that. All they bring me is headaches.

SARAH. (*Passing Joshua his tea.*) You say that every summer.

JOSHUA. Thank ya, Mrs. Webber. Gorry, I never seen so many people in my life.

SARAH. Well, I suppose it's all the young people coming back now that the wars are over.

JOSHUA. If that's the case, Mrs. Webber, General MacArthur musta found a way to split 'em all inta twins. Ayuh . . . right clever trick for a war, but it don't do much for peace. (*Sips tea.*) Y' know, there was an accident last week down by the Post Office. First one ever.

SARAH. You don't say.

TISHA. I hadn't heard.

JOSHUA. I was right there. Some damn summer complaint from Connecticut run over young Harvey Randall's foot.

SARAH. Oh, my . . .

JOSHUA. 'T'weren't too serious, mind ya, but it's a sign of things to come.

SARAH. There certainly is more traffic.

JOSHUA. Ayuh, I never seen so damn many cars in my life. Some of these summer people bring down two. Lord knows

28

why . . . I don't need even one. Ya can't walk more'n a mile 'fore ya fall inta the ocean.

TISHA. It'll quiet down soon enough, Joshua.

JOSHUA. Ayuh. Good thing, September.

TISHA. (*After a slight pause.*) Helen Parsons told me you were seein' Myrtle Jackson again.

JOSHUA. Ayuh . . . when I can, when I can.

SARAH. I'm glad to hear it.

TISHA. Ayuh, you two make a lovely couple.

JOSHUA. Well, Myrtle's a *lady*, Mrs. Doughty. She knows how to get gussied up. Ayuh, she don't go paradin' around like a livin' beach ball all squeezed inta Bermud-ee shorts . . .

SARAH. (*She and Tisha chuckle.*) Oh Joshua . . .

JOSHUA. I quit a job on a woman like that, last week. Left m' tools right there.

TISHA. You went back for 'em, I hope.

JOSHUA. I got plenty o' tools, Mrs. Doughty, but I got no time for people like that.

SARAH. What happened, Joshua?

JOSHUA. People like that won't even pass the time o' day with ya, won't even offer ya a cup o' tea. (*Slight pause.*) Oh, they can hire young Eddie Wentworth and his *vo*-cational certificates, but the work'll fall apart in two years, I'll tell ya. Ayuh, when them people figure out it takes time to make somethin' good, I'll be gone and they'll be out o' luck right proper!

TISHA. Joshua . . . you haven't told us what happened.

JOSHUA. (*Pause.*) She told me I was too slow, Mrs. Doughty.

TISHA. The idea!

JOSHUA. Well, I told her to get somebody else if she thought she'd get better. I ain't been back.

SARAH. Good for you.

TISHA. That'll show 'em.

JOSHUA. Ayuh. (*Pause while he finishes his tea.*) Y'know, I can't imagine what I'd do if I retired . . .

29

TISHA. 'Course y' can't. And what would we do if y' did?

JOSHUA. Well, I'd do neighborly favors for you ladies anyway.

SARAH. You're a kind man, Joshua.

JOSHUA. There's some that wouldn't agree.

TISHA. They just don't know you.

JOSHUA. *Won't*, neither. (*Pause.*) We're seein' the future, ladies. Don't like it much. (*Rises, puts on cap.*) Well, mighty nice cup o' tea. Best this end of the island.

SARAH. Joshua Brackett, you are a flatterer.

JOSHUA. Ayuh . . . that, too. (*Gathers tool box.*) You made up your mind about that new picture window we talked about? I can get ya a nice price on the lumber right now.

SARAH. I don't know, Joshua. Libby thinks we're too far along to be trying something new for the cottage.

JOSHUA. (*Exiting into bathroom.*) Nothin' wrong with new, Mrs. Webber, if it makes somethin' good better. (*Closes bathroom door behind him with a slam.*)

SARAH. Oh, Joshua . . . (*Rises and moves D. toward "windows" at C.*) It's whale time, Tisha. The herring are running.

TISHA. Ayuh. I've seen the fishermen's spotter planes out over the bay.

SARAH. Remember how many there used to be?

TISHA. Gorry, I remember when there weren't *any*. So do you.

SARAH. I mean whales, Tisha, not planes.

TISHA. Oh.

SARAH. The very first summer we met, we watched the whales together. You kept grabbing the glasses from me.

TISHA. Well, you were piggy with 'em. Still are. (*Joins Sarah D.*) Ayuh, whales and Northern Lights. I saw the Lights last week. The Maine coast is tellin' us summer's a goner.

SARAH. Yes . . . but not 'til the whales come. How nice we still watch them together every year.

TISHA. Ayuh . . .

SARAH. I wish there were as many as before the war.

TISHA. Which war, dear?

SARAH. The last one.

TISHA. I expect all those German submarines scared 'em away.

SARAH. Oh, you and your German submarines. I never did put much stock in 'em.

TISHA. No, you didn't, but I saw 'em several times — 'specially in Forty-two.

SARAH. They were never verified.

TISHA. Well, those Coastal Watchers — or whatever they were called — *never* followed up on my sightin's.

SARAH. Perhaps because you saw too many, dear?

TISHA. Good Heavens, Sarah! In war time, you can't be too careful.

SARAH. You know, I haven't seen any porpoises.

TISHA. Ayuh, and nary a seal.

SARAH. They say the water temperature has something to do with it.

TISHA. If y' ask me, it's the Russians. They've got the bomb. There's no tellin' what else they're up to.

SARAH. (*Pause.*) Do you suppose we still might find some ambergris?

TISHA. My land! I haven't thought about our ambergris hunts for years!

SARAH. We were going to make our fortunes.

TISHA. Ayuh . . . the new perfume queens. Ten dollars an *ounce* that stuff was! Weren't we the pair?

SARAH. Yes . . . poking around Whaleback Cove all those afternoons —

TISHA. Oh, yes —

SARAH. Keeping just ahead of the tide, loaded down with our rocks —

TISHA. 'Cause we knew for a fact that every sperm whale in the ocean had come into the bay to vomit — just for us!

SARAH. Yes . . . and there was that time we ran into all

31

those proper ladies from the Knickerbocker Hotel —

TISHA. They were goin' to the Inn for tea —

SARAH. And Mrs. Miltimore was right in the middle of them —

TISHA. That old snoot!

SARAH. And when you said hello, you dropped your whole load of rocks smack on her foot!

TISHA. And the only thing she said was, "My dear Miss Benson, will you kindly tell us what you girls are doing?" Girls?! We were thirty if we were a day!

SARAH. I couldn't look at you!

TISHA. "This is ambergris, Mrs. Miltimore, enough to make us millionaires."

SARAH. "My de-ah young lady, look again. Your treasure is merely pumice stone."

TISHA. An old snoot with eyes like a sparrow hawk —

SARAH. I *never* forgave her for ruining our dreams.

TISHA. Well, at least I got seaweed on her lily-white shoes!! (*Tisha bursts into laughter and Sarah joins her.*)

LIBBY. (*Re-awakened by the laughter within.*) Sarah? Sarah!

SARAH. I nearly forgot . . . (*Crosses to porch door.*) Tisha's here. Will you come in and join us?

LIBBY. I expect I've had enough sun. (*Rises and goes toward door.*)

SARAH. (*Holding door open for Libby.*) Will you have some tea?

LIBBY. No, Sarah. (*Enters living room, crosses toward platform rocker.*)

TISHA. Libby Strong, you're lookin' younger every day.

LIBBY. Hmmph.

TISHA. Yes indeedy, like a stout oak, dear.

LIBBY. You two were certainly carrying on. (*Sits in platform rocker.*)

SARAH. We were laughing about our old ambergris hunts.

TISHA. (*Getting berry pail and crossing to Libby.*) I brought you some blackberries, Libby. (*Extends pail for Libby to taste one.*) Gorry, what a walk to find so few berries! I swear there aren't as many as there used to be.

LIBBY. It's those nuns.

TISHA. Nuns, Libby?

LIBBY. That's what I said. They flock around our blueberries like a bunch of penguins.

TISHA. Well, nuns are entitled to pick berries, too.

LIBBY. Not in our woods.

SARAH. Oh, for pity's sake, Libby.

TISHA. (*Taking a seat.*) Girls, I do have some news. (*Expectant pause.*) Helen Parsons told me that Hilda Partridge passed away yesterday at the Medical Center.

SARAH. Oh, no . . .

TISHA. Ayuh. They took her off-island on the fireboat just the day before.

LIBBY. We hadn't even heard she was ill.

TISHA. Very sudden it was . . . and mercifully quick for her.

SARAH. Hilda was so young . . .

LIBBY. I know for a fact she was eighty-three.

TISHA. I had no idea. (*Slight pause.*) Y' know, Mr. Maranov's been stayin' at Hilda's this summer.

SARAH. What will he do now?

LIBBY. Yes, whom will he grace?

SARAH. Libby . . .

TISHA. Helen said he was still there as of today, but she wasn't sure about his plans.

SARAH. (*A small sigh.*) When is the funeral?

TISHA. Monday comin', in Portland.

SARAH. Which home?

TISHA. Nulty and Sons.

LIBBY. That's a Catholic home!

TISHA. Hilda's daughter married one, and I guess he's makin' the arrangements.

LIBBY. When my time comes, Sarah, don't you dare—

33

SARAH. I know, dear, I know.

TISHA. I'm sure gonna miss Hilda. She was a crackerjack bridge partner. (*Pause.*) Oh, you'll never guess who finally bought a hearin' aid!

SARAH. Who, dear?

TISHA. Alice Trueworthy. Ayuh, and now she's become our duplicate champion. (*Pause.*) I bet she never heard the biddin' before. (*They all share the laugh.*)

SARAH. We received a lovely note from Lydia Frothingham.

TISHA. Is the hip mendin'?

SARAH. Not well at all.

LIBBY. You know how it is with hips. She'll be meeting him soon.

TISHA. Meetin' who, dear?

LIBBY. The escort.

SARAH. (*Quickly turning the conversation.*) Have you seen anything of Charlie Mayhew lately?

TISHA. You haven't heard?

SARAH. What?

TISHA. He up and married that young waitress from the Abenaki House.

SARAH. You don't say!

TISHA. I do say. Scandalous!

LIBBY. But not surprising. The late Mrs. Mayhew could have taken the booby prize at a cattle show.

SARAH. Libby!

TISHA. Libby Strong, what a team you and Fred Allen would make! (*Slight pause.*) Still, Betty Mayhew's grave hardly has grass on it.

SARAH. How's your arthritis, dear?

TISHA. In again, out again, gone again Finnegan . . . you know.

SARAH. That's too bad, dear.

TISHA. Well, my young doctor told me to expect it if I was determined to live so long.

SARAH. He needs a lesson in bedside manners.

TISHA. Oh, he's so cute, dear, I can forgive him almost anythin'. (*Maranov appears on porch boardwalk. Unbowed by his years, he moves with grace and dignity. He wears woolen knickers — a rather worn, dark tweed — stout boots and heavy socks, a blue shirt, and a roomy, old navy blue cardigan, all rather comfortably gone to seed. He sports a Panama hat and carries a bamboo fishing pole along with his burlap-bagged catch of sea perch. The women don't notice him as he approaches the screened door.*)

SARAH. Have you sewn anything for the Fair?

TISHA. What with one thing and another, I haven't had time this year.

MARANOV. (*At screen door.*) Mrs. Webber? Mrs. Strong?

SARAH. (*Rising.*) It's Mr. Maranov!

LIBBY. My glasses, Sarah!

SARAH. Really, dear, you don't —

LIBBY. I must have them! You get my glasses. Tisha can let him in. (*Tisha nods assent to Sarah; Sarah exits to Libby's bedroom while Tisha primps briefly and then goes to porch door.*)

TISHA. (*Opening door and standing in entrance.*) Mr. Maranov, please come in.

MARANOV. Mrs. Doughty, what an unexpected pleasure! How lovely you look today!

TISHA. I'll remember you in my will. Now, come in, come in.

MARANOV. I fear these creatures will become odorous if I leave them . . . (*Sarah enters from Libby's bedroom, crosses to Libby to deliver dark glasses — which Libby hastily dons — and moves toward the screen door.*)

SARAH. Mr. Maranov, you bring those fish right in and I'll put them on ice.

MARANOV. You are so kind. (*Enters, doffing hat and extending his catch to Sarah who has hurried to greet him.*) They are a rather good catch, eh?

SARAH. (*Feeling the heft of the fish.*) Oh my, yes. Please, find a seat while I take care of these. (*Exits to kitchen.*)

MARANOV. Ah, Mrs. Strong . . . it is a pleasure to see you again. (*Executes a courtly bow.*)

LIBBY. Thank you, sir.

TISHA. He's the only man left alive who still bows.

MARANOV. An old habit, madame.

TISHA. And a charmin' one.

MARANOV. It is my nod to gentler times . . and, to present company. (*Sits.*)

SARAH. (*Entering from kitchen.*) I'm so glad you stopped by, Mr. Maranov.

MARANOV. I, too, Mrs. Webber. I am having a splendid morning. A successful fishing expedition in the hot sun and, now, refreshing company.

JOSHUA. (*Opening bathroom door with a bang.*) I got her all caulked up good, Mrs. Webber. (*Everyone starts, and Maranov begins to rise.*) Don't ya move an inch, Mr. Maranov. I already know you're a gentleman. (*Tips cap to the ladies.*) I'd stay for the party but I got to run 'round the point to see what Helen Parsons is yellin' about. Gorry, that woman's got more problems than Mrs. Roosevelt's got causes. (*Crossing to kitchen.*) You think about that picture window, ladies. You let me do it, and the view might even keep Mr. Maranov from jumpin' up every time somebody moves—

SARAH. I'll show you out, Joshua.

JOSHUA. No, no . . . I know the way. (*Exits.*)

TISHA. Are you goin' to put in the new window?

LIBBY. It would be too expensive.

TISHA. Libby Strong, it'd be worth every penny. Why, you wouldn't have to move an inch in this room to see the moon come up.

MARANOV. I must agree with Mr. Brackett. It would make a magnificent addition.

LIBBY. We'd get very little use out of it.

TISHA. It's a shame it's not in already.

MARANOV. Yes, imagine . . . to dine and be flooded by moonlight.

LIBBY. We're too far along to be trying something new for the cottage.

TISHA. Ayuh, a right shame . . . the moon's gonna be full tonight . . .

MARANOV. Alas . . . I shall not see it from my room on the bayside.

SARAH. Mr. Maranov . . .

MARANOV. Yes, Mrs. Webber?

SARAH. If you would consider cleaning those fish, I'll bake them. Will you then join us for dinner *and* moonrise?

MARANOV. Mrs. Webber, how kind of you to offer. Indeed, I shall be most happy to donate my catch and my filleting technique to our dinner.

LIBBY. I will not eat those fish!

SARAH. Now Libby—

LIBBY. (*Quickly. Covering her gaffe.*) It's the bones. I've always been afraid of fish bones.

MARANOV. They do warrant your caution, madame.

SARAH. Tisha, can you join us for dinner, too?

TISHA. Well, dear, I wish I could, but I promised Helen Parsons I'd visit for the evening.

SARAH. Oh, too bad, dear.

TISHA. Another time, Sarah.

SARAH. I have a splendid idea! Tomorrow morning, we could all watch the whales together!

MARANOV. How exciting!

SARAH. It's time for them. In fact, they're late arriving this year.

MARANOV. You know, I have never seen them.

SARAH. It's settled then? You'll come down in the morning?

MARANOV. Indeed, Mrs. Webber.

TISHA. Well . . . all right, dear.

SARAH. Good. I'll put your blackberries into my favorite

37

muffins and we'll have a little picnic on the porch while we watch the whales.

LIBBY. Don't cool the muffins on the windowsill. The nuns might snatch them.

TISHA. Libby Strong, what a card!

SARAH. (*After a slight pause.*) Mr. Maranov . . . we were very sorry to hear about Hilda's death. Please accept our condolences.

MARANOV. Thank you, Mrs. Webber.

TISHA. She was a good friend to us all.

MARANOV. Yes. We shall miss her very much.

TISHA. I guess you must be all discombobulated right now . . .

MARANOV. Somewhat, my dear. But, I have spent my fishing time well, and my thoughts are more orderly than before. (*Brief pause.*) Let us not speak of sad things. Mrs. Doughty, how is your little Pekinese? Ah . . . what is it you call him?

TISHA. T'ing Hao . . . my little Dingey. Well, he's a bit crippled by the arthritis.

MARANOV. Poor little fellow . . .

TISHA. He's almost thirteen, y' know. I have to carry him up and down stairs.

MARANOV. That must be a burden for you, my dear.

TISHA. Oh, no burden, Mr. Maranov. He fills up the house for me. It's a fair exchange.

MARANOV. Yes, of course. Do you still take him motoring with you? I have not seen you lately behind the wheel of your Model A.

TISHA. It's in my garage.

SARAH. Oh yes, dear. What *did* happen?

TISHA. They wouldn't tell me. I tried to ask 'em, but they wouldn't tell me.

MARANOV. Who—

TISHA. They were givin' 'em out right and left that day, I'll tell ya. There was young woman there and she got a pink slip, too. I asked her why, but they wouldn't tell her either.

MARANOV. How very odd.

TISHA. No use tryin' to talk to those people—not a word, a word! I left right away, I'll tell ya.

SARAH. But, dear—

TISHA. I still drive. I do. Oh, not 'round the corner for a visit, mind ya. But . . I *do* drive.

MARANOV. Should you, my dear?

TISHA. To the market and the Post Office can't hurt. I've been drivin' since nineteen and ten and *never* had an accident! (*Pause.*) A little bump when the examiner told me to back up. What's a little bump, I ask ya?

SARAH. Dear . . did you lose your license?

TISHA. A suspension it was . . .

MARANOV. Then all is not lost, dear lady.

TISHA. They told me I could try again in six months. (*Pause.*) Well . . . well. Six months . . . six months is . . . a very long time. (*Near tears, but fighting them.*)

MARANOV. (*After a brief pause.*) Ah, Mrs. Doughty, the pedestrian state is good for the circulation.

TISHA. It's the inconvenience, don't y' see . . . the damned inconvenience.

MARANOV. Only a diversion, madame, a temporary change in status. Mrs. Doughty, traffic will come to a full halt when you are seen standing by the roadside, thumb extended . . . provocative, mysterious, alluring.

TISHA. Oh, Mr. Maranov, you're a caution.

SARAH. You'll have your license back in no time, dear.

TISHA. Gracious! My Dingey must be right hungry by now. I'll have to go. (*Rises.*)

MARANOV. I pass your cottage on my way. May I offer you my arm as your carriage home?

TISHA. Ayuh, my last cavalier, you may. (*Maranov and Sarah rise.*) Oh, the dear. She's catnappin'.

SARAH. She had quite a bit of sun. I'll see you out.

MARANOV. Nothing of the sort, Mrs. Webber. If we all

leave, the silence will awaken her. (*He and Tisha move toward door, Tisha leading.*) Mrs. Webber, when shall I return to prepare our fish?

SARAH. Come down around five-thirty, Mr. Maranov.

MARANOV. (*A slight bow to Sarah.*) Until then, madame.

TISHA. Bye, Sarah. See you in the mornin', dear.

SARAH. Bye, dear. (*Maranov and Tisha exit to porch, where he reclaims his fishing pole and puts on his hat.*)

TISHA. My, I must've got cooled down sittin' so long.

MARANOV. In another place and time, I would offer my cape to warm you.

TISHA. There's my Sir Walter again.

MARANOV. (*Removes his sweater.*) My dear . . . please . . .

TISHA. Oh, I couldn't, Mr. Maranov.

MARANOV. You must, my dear.

TISHA. Oh, no . . .

MARANOV. My dear, at the very least, wear it to ward off the hot breath of your ancient, doomed cavalier.

TISHA. Oh . . . my, my . . . drape me then! (*He drapes her shoulders with his sweater; they exit on boardwalk.*)

SLOW FADE TO BLACK

ACT I

Scene 3

Late afternoon of the same day. The sun has westered, leaving the porch in shadow. Libby sits in her platform rocker, tapping her feet in a private rhythm. Sarah's apron project remains unfinished on the dining table. The clatter of dishes is heard in the kitchen.

SARAH. (*Enters from kitchen with three place settings of china and silverware.*) Libby, aren't you changed yet? Mr. Maranov will be here shortly.

LIBBY. This is the mauve dress, isn't it?

SARAH. (*Putting dishes on the dining table.*) I still have a lot to do. If you get ready now, I'll have time to make sure you're all proper for Mr. Maranov.

LIBBY. He's not my guest.

SARAH. He's *our* guest, dear. (*Arranging table setting, clearing apron things to side table.*)

LIBBY. I didn't invite him, and I don't want his fish.

SARAH. I'm giving you a pork chop. Dear, he'll be here in less than an hour.

LIBBY. He'll be here for the rest of your life if you let him.

SARAH. (*Exiting to kitchen.*) Oh, Libby . . .

LIBBY. This is the mauve dress, isn't it?

SARAH. (*Off.*) What, dear?

LIBBY. I asked you if this were the mauve dress!

SARAH. (*Off.*) Yes, it is.

LIBBY. Then it's perfectly suitable for dinner.

SARAH. (*Entering with napkins in rings.*) Libby, time is running out.

LIBBY. "Last night I saw upon the stair . . ."

SARAH. I'm running behind schedule.

LIBBY. "A little man who wasn't there . . ."

SARAH. I haven't got time to waste, Libby.

LIBBY. "He wasn't there again today . . ."

SARAH. Libby . . .

LIBBY. "Oh, how I wish he'd go away."

SARAH. Why don't you put on your green dress?

LIBBY. I'm not going to change at all.

SARAH. (*Exiting to kitchen.*) Well, if you don't want to join our little party . . .

LIBBY. What are we celebrating?

SARAH. (*Entering with water glasses.*) Libby, please. I have to finish the table, I have to get dressed, and the muffins for the morning are almost done.

LIBBY. Busy, busy . . . always busy.

SARAH. I haven't even finished the aprons . . .

LIBBY. Start to choose, Sarah.

SARAH. What?

LIBBY. Like Tisha. She chose to lose her license.

SARAH. You can't mean that.

LIBBY. She decided she didn't want to drive anymore. One thing follows another.

SARAH. Nonsense.

LIBBY. Call it what you will. Everything's some kind of nonsense. (*Pause.*) Whisper "cataracts" to yourself and see what happens.

SARAH. My God, Libby!

LIBBY. Nothing remarkable about it when you've seen everything you wanted to.

SARAH. That's preposterous.

LIBBY. I'm working on my ears now.

SARAH. I don't want to hear it.

LIBBY. Oh . . . working on *your* ears?

SARAH. Enough, Libby.

LIBBY. What will you shut down, Sarah?

SARAH. Nothing, Elizabeth Mae. Now, you *must* dress.

LIBBY. I will not change for him.

SARAH. Why not?

LIBBY. He is a stranger.

SARAH. He is a guest.

LIBBY. Strangers are not welcome.

SARAH. They are when we need them.

LIBBY. What are you planning, Sarah Louise?

SARAH. Nothing.

LIBBY. Oh yes, you are!

SARAH. I have only invited Mr. Maranov to dinner.

LIBBY. We don't need him in this house.

SARAH. Elizabeth Mae, Mr. Maranov is a part of the world that *I* am still *in*.

LIBBY. *We're* the world, and it's complete!

SARAH. I have no time for this.

LIBBY. You never *have* time. You *make* time!

SARAH. No, Libby.

LIBBY. When Mother died, *I* made the time. I took care of you.

SARAH. You did what you had to do.

LIBBY. Yes, I did! (*Pause.*) You owe me. (*Pause.*) I did it. I did it for fifteen years!

SARAH. Then we're even! Fifteen years for fifteen years! (*Exits to kitchen.*)

LIBBY. Come back here, Sarah Louise! You come back here! Don't you run away, child!

SARAH. (*Off.*) Oh, damn! The muffins have burned! Look what you made me do!

LIBBY. (*Rising and groping her way toward kitchen.*) Now, Sarah Louise . . . let's not fight, dear. Let's be good and not

43

fight anymore. Never mind the muffins, dear.

SARAH. (*Entering and moving just into the living room to face Libby.*) I will not let you ruin dinner. Get dressed and let me finish what I have to do.

LIBBY. It's *done*. Don't you see? (*Pause.*) Sarah . . . do you remember how every summer we went into the woods and tied strips of cloth to the tree branches to mark all the trails between here and there so we could always find our way even when the trails grew over? (*Slight pause.*) We're meant to share that now. Help me gather the cloth strips, Sarah Louise. Don't be so busy that we miss the chance.

SARAH. That's not living.

LIBBY. It's what's left to us. (*Pause.*) I only dream of Death, Sarah, because He dreams of me.

SARAH. We're so very different, you and I.

LIBBY. We're *blood*, Sarah Louise. And there's so little time left for kindness.

FAST FADE TO BLACK

END, ACT I

ACT II

Scene 1

It is the gentle, windless time of day when sea birds go home to roost and the ocean stills for sunset. End-of-sunset colours stream in through the window behind Libby's platform rocker and wash the set from L. Waves lap on the rocks below; the bell buoy rings occasionally; a very few gull cries break the stillness. As the scene progresses, the colours fade to twilight grey and into night darkness. Eventually, moonrise will brighten the darkness.

The Tiffany style lamp is lighted. Maranov and Libby are seated at table, while Sarah clears the last of the dinner dishes. Maranov wears an old, somewhat faded blue-and-white striped seersucker suit and white shirt and dark tie; Sarah no longer wears her hair net and wears a dress more suitable for dinner. Libby has changed into her green dress, after all, and it is in the same style as her mauve dress.

MARANOV. (*In mid-story as the lights come up.*) But in the winters when we came back to St. Petersburg, it was the Grand Duke who gave the most elegant entertainments. Yes, imagine if you will three hundred couples swirling around the ballroom in a Viennese waltz . . . ah, the ladies in their gowns rose and fell but never seemed to touch the floor . . . (*Slight pause.*) Mrs. Strong, I have been remiss in not complimenting you upon your dinner dress. It is most becoming to you.

LIBBY. Thank you, sir.

MARANOV. You are welcome, madame. (*Pause, while he listens to the sounds.*) Even though we have no orchestra, we are indeed fortunate to dine with the sounds of the sea.

SARAH. (*Taking her seat again.*) Mmm . . . and its music is ever-changing, isn't it?

MARANOV. Indeed, Mrs. Webber. But then, a thing of beauty is never fully at rest.

SARAH. Mr. Maranov, you have an excellent filleting technique. I didn't find a single bone.

MARANOV. Thank you, my dear. But I regret, Mrs. Strong, that you did not share our bounty.

LIBBY. My pork chop was excellent.

SARAH. Shall we take our coffee on the porch?

MARANOV. That would be delightful.

SARAH. (*Rising and going to kitchen.*) Why don't you both enjoy the air while I get the coffee? I do hope we can do this again before Labor Day . . . (*Exits into kitchen.*)

MARANOV. (*Rising.*) I, too, Mrs. Webber. (*Stands by to assist Libby who obviously doesn't want help.*) Labor Day is such a sad holiday, Mrs. Strong. It drives us home to our winter caves.

LIBBY. And where will you hibernate, Mr. Maranov?

MARANOV. (*While holding porch door open for Libby.*) I shall probably rent a small flat on the mainland.

LIBBY. A rather long way from St. Petersburg . . .

MARANOV. Yes, Mrs. Strong, but almost as cold.

LIBBY. (*Sitting.*) I should think you'd find your way south for the winter.

MARANOV. One makes economies, madame.

LIBBY. I suspected you were a . . . practical man.

MARANOV. A primary requisite for a long life, would you not agree?

LIBBY. (*Nods assent.*) But practicalities shift, do they not?

46

MARANOV. I beg your pardon, Mrs. Strong? (*Sarah nears porch door with coffee tray and overhears Libby's next line.*)

LIBBY. I mean, sir, one makes adjustments according to circumstances, don't you agree?

MARANOV. (*Moving away toward his seat.*) Of course, madame.

SARAH. (*Entering and crossing to side table.*) I'm so glad you came, Mr. Maranov. After all, how often does one get a chance to entertain a member of the Russian Imperial Court?

MARANOV. (*Sits, then answers.*) These days, my dear . . . never.

SARAH. (*Serving coffee to Libby.*) You're too modest. Once a nobleman, always a nobleman.

MARANOV. Ah, Mrs. Webber, that is all past tense now. My estate has changed.

SARAH. (*Bringing tray to him for his selection of cream and sugar.*) Well, life at the Tsar's court must have been splendid.

MARANOV. It was not always that, my dear.

SARAH. (*Setting tray on side table and pouring her own cup.*) Oh, but Helen Parsons has told me of your photographs, especially the one at Court with your mother wearing a magnificent velvet gown, all trimmed in ermine!

MARANOV. Yes . . . at the Winter Palace, nineteen and ten, I believe.

SARAH. (*Taking her seat.*) I'd love to see those photographs someday.

MARANOV. I hope you will, my dear. But, alas, my photographs are insufficient images.

LIBBY. No photograph can be as rich as a single memory.

MARANOV. True, madame, but I fear my memories are imperfect as well.

LIBBY. Then you must work at them, sir. You will lose them if you don't search them out.

MARANOV. I prefer serendipity, madame. Your hair, for example. When I look upon it, suddenly I remember the ermine that trimmed my Mother's winter gowns. (*Pause.*) Yes

. . . your tresses recall more than any photograph could. (*Slight pause.*) But, I suppose that after a certain point in our lives, everything is reminiscent of something else.

SARAH. Oh my . . . caught among philosophers.

MARANOV. The price you pay for such a splendid repast.

SARAH. It was hardly that. I'm sure our dinner didn't match the grandeur of a Grand Duke's feast.

MARANOV. Dear lady, I must assure you that I have learned that all board is precious, and all company . . grand.

SARAH. We may have to remember you in our wills if you go on this way.

MARANOV. Unnecessary, madame, but I do hope you will remember me next summer at mackerel season.

SARAH. It's a promise.

LIBBY. It's getting dark, isn't it?

MARANOV. There's still a bit of light, madame.

LIBBY. The days are noticeably shorter.

MARANOV. Indeed they are. We are perched on autumn's precipice.

LIBBY. Yes . . . it will be November before we know it.

SARAH. Mr. Maranov, won't you tell us a bit about Paris after all of you got out of Russia.

MARANOV. All of us did not "get out." (*Sees Sarah's discomfort.*) No-no-no . . . I did not mean to reprove. (*Pause.*) Ah . . . Paris . . . yes . . .

SARAH. Those must have been dashing times!

MARANOV. In their way, my dear.

LIBBY. There's not much excitement here, Mr. Maranov.

MARANOV. Ah, but Mrs. Strong, here there is true excitement. We have the promise of moonrise and whales.

SARAH. But in Paris with all that royalty around, it must have been like living in a swirl of champagne bubbles.

MARANOV. (*With an amused chuckle.*) Well, we of the noble diaspora did sparkle for a time before we settled into the sooty surface. (*Pause.*) Yes . . . we had our parties and our plots, and our obligatory visits to the Dowager Empress.

48

We managed to nourish our dreams for a while. (*Pause.*) Nevertheless, mesdames, we were merely . . . bijoux . . . little human trinkets, exquisitely embellished to be sure . . . but purely ornamental. (*Pause.*) Trinkets, yes. For each other's hopes and amusements.

SARAH. I had no idea . . .

MARANOV. Few of us did, either. (*Slight pause.*) All tribes doomed by progress suffer from subtle ailments preliminary to their extinctions.

LIBBY. But you are not extinct, Mr. Maranov.

MARANOV. No. I am still very much here.

LIBBY. Indeed. (*Pause.*) Where have you been staying this summer, Mr. Maranov?

SARAH. Libby, he was staying with Hilda Partridge.

LIBBY. Of course, I had forgotten.

MARANOV. Yes, I was her guest . . . until she was so unexpectedly taken from us.

LIBBY. Poor Hilda . . . and how terribly unfortunate for you.

MARANOV. It is a grievous loss for all of us, madame.

LIBBY. Yes. (*Slight pause.*) Where have you . . . relocated, Mr. Maranov?

MARANOV. (*Pause.*) I have not yet done so, Mrs. Strong. Mrs. Partridge's daughter has given me leave of the cottage until the day after the funeral.

LIBBY. Then you have three more days.

MARANOV. Yes.

SARAH. Libby . . .

LIBBY. Will you be able to attend the funeral, or will other . . . practicalities interfere?

SARAH. Libby, I'm quite sure Mr. Maranov would rather not dwell on this.

MARANOV. Mrs. Strong . . . for nearly a decade, Hilda Partridge was my very dear friend. (*Slight pause.*) I will honour her and I will attend her last rites.

LIBBY. The night chill has come on. I believe I'll retire.

(*Rises and goes to porch door.*) Good night, all. (*Enters living room, crosses to her bedroom, enters it, closes door behind her.*)

SARAH. (*Rises and crosses to Maranov who has risen for Libby's exit.*) Mr. Maranov . . . I'm so terribly sorry.

MARANOV. Your sister is a . . . remarkable woman. (*Pause.*) She does not make small talk.

SARAH. Her behaviour is unforgiveable!

MARANOV. No, my dear. I should not have come to your door this morning.

SARAH. Nonsense, Mr. Maranov.

MARANOV. No. Truth. (*Pause.*) I followed the instinct of a great many years . . . and your very astute sister recognized it.

SARAH. Whatever do you mean, Mr. Maranov?

MARANOV. (*Long pause.*) Mrs. Webber . . . in three days time, I shall have no place to go. I shall be once again . . . set adrift.

SARAH. I see, Mr. Maranov. (*Pause.*) I had imagined your life filled with many people.

MARANOV. I have myself, my dear. As for the rest, a great many years have used them up.

SARAH. Yes . . . (*Slight pause.*) I'm very sorry, Mr. Maranov.

MARANOV. You needn't be, my dear. I have often been adrift, but I have always stayed afloat.

SARAH. (*Pause.*) It must take a great deal of courage to go on so . . . alone.

MARANOV. No, not courage, my dear. Nothing so heroic as that. No . . . merely a considerable investment of will.

SARAH. If I were to be . . . alone, I don't think I'd possess the will.

MARANOV. My dear, it lurks here, inside. One needs only to search it out.

SARAH. How did you find it, Mr. Maranov?

MARANOV. (*Pause.*) It was in Paris, after the Dowager Empress died. We were all in deep mourning and my mother had not spoken to anyone for over a week. Then, one morning, she called me into her sitting room. "Nikolai," she said, "Marie Federovna is gone. There will be no more use for us. You may leave me now. Go into the world at large." And then, my dear, she presented me a handkerchief in which she had wrapped nearly all her jewels, and she insisted I take them. (*Pause.*) Yes, my mother kissed me and said, "Use my treasure as you need, but at the end, my son, be able to say it was well spent." (*Withdraws a handkerchief from his pocket and unwraps it to reveal a large emerald, surrounded by diamonds, in a heavy Victorian setting. He holds the ring out to Sarah.*) This is the last.

SARAH. How lovely . . .

MARANOV. It should fetch quite enough to carry me 'cross the bar. (*A pause while he puts the ring back in his pocket.*)

SARAH. Your mother was a remarkable woman, Mr. Maranov.

MARANOV. Yes, she was.

SARAH. She gave you an extraordinary gift.

MARANOV. Yes, she did.

SARAH. I don't mean the jewels.

MARANOV. I know.

SARAH. She gave you your life.

MARANOV. For the second time, my dear. She knew that the first was over.

SARAH. Yes, and she let you begin anew.

MARANOV. And I have been doing just that ever since.

SARAH. I envy you. You have been free, Mr. Maranov.

MARANOV. Mrs. Webber, I have found you out! You are a romanticist.

SARAH. Oh, I don't know about that . . .

MARANOV. Yes, my dear, you are. But you forget that I am once again adrift, on this sea of freedom that you envy.

SARAH. (*A long pause.*) . . . Do you think that one can live too long?

51

MARANOV. Mrs. Webber, life can *never* be too long.

SARAH. Even if one . . . outlives one's time?

MARANOV. No, my dear. One's time is *all* one's time, even to the end.

SARAH. (*Long pause. She goes to porch rail to face the sea.*) Look . . . there's the moon, Mr. Maranov.

MARANOV. (*Joining her at the rail.*) How magnificent . . . my dear, you have kept your promise. (*Pause.*) Do you see how the moon casts silver coins along the shore? There is a treasure, my dear, that can never be spent.

SARAH. Oh! (*Pause.*) On my wedding night, my husband said to me, "Can you imagine being old, my love? Whatever shall we do when our passion's spent?"

MARANOV. Did you reply?

SARAH. I said, "We shall buy some more."

MARANOV. Well spoken, Mrs. Webber! Well spoken indeed. Your husband was a very fortunate man.

SARAH. (*Pause.*) What of love, Mr. Maranov? Surely you have loved?

MARANOV. (*Slight pause.*) Some pretty profiles under street lamps . . . yes. Finite liaisons in darkened rooms across two continents . . . yes, But, love, my dear? No.

SARAH. (*Pause.*) Forgive me, Mr. Maranov, but I must try to know. (*Slight pause.*) All these years, from St. Petersburg to Maine, what has it been? What have you done?

MARANOV. (*Pause.*) I have spent my life . . . visiting friends. (*Long pause.*) I should be on my way.

SARAH. Will you be able to keep our morning appointment?

MARANOV. I think it would be best if I did not.

SARAH. I understand.

MARANOV. Thank you, my dear. (*Bows to her.*) Mrs. Webber . . . I shall treasure this night forever.

SARAH. You will always be my welcome guest, Mr. Maranov.

MARANOV. (*Turns from her to move toward exit on board-*

walk.) Sleep well. You have your engagement with leviathans, madame, and it would not do to keep them waiting. (*He pauses briefly to look at the moon, then exits U. on boardwalk. Sarah gathers coffee things on tray, picks up tray and faces the moon for a moment.*)

SARAH. So . . . here I am . . . adrift. (*She turns and enters living room, crossing to kitchen to deposit tray, while the lights fade slowly to:.*)

BLACK

ACT II

Scene 2

In the scene break while Sarah changes her costume, the lights come up again: a strip of light spills out from under Sarah's bedroom door, and moonlight floods the porch and streams into the living room from R. The sea surges softly outside and the bell buoy mournfully punctuates the stillness.

Sarah opens her bedroom door and is silhouetted for a moment in the light from behind her. She is formally dressed in a gown of Thirties vintage, a floor-length blue-grey dress, embroidered at the bodice with tiny, deep-blue beads that catch and contain the light. She closes the door behind her and crosses to a cupboard (dining area) where she opens a drawer and removes a white linen tablecloth. She crosses then to the small table in the cluster arrangement below the fireplace, moves the table D.C. into moonlight streaming from R., and spreads the the cloth over the table.

*She crosses to the cupboard again and takes from it
to the table a cut glass wine decanter (with red wine)
and one cut glass wine goblet. She then crosses up to
mantel and removes from it the tall candlestick and
its white taper, and the photograph of Philip, which
she then places carefully on the small table. Then she
returns to the mantel for matches, carries them back
to the table, strikes a light, and lights the taper.*

*This done, she lays the matches aside and goes to the
kitchen, from which she returns with a slender cut
glass vase in which are the single red rose and single
white rose we saw in the first moments of the play.
She places the vase on the small table and briefly
studies her arrangement, making small adjustments
here and there. Satisfied, she pulls a chair to the
table, then pours her wine with almost reverent cere-
mony. At last, she sits, facing D., with the photograph turned to face her.*

SARAH. Forty-two, Philip. (*Pause.*) The forty-second red
rose, the forty-second white. (*She raises her glass, dips it to
the photo, and sips.*) White for truth, red for passion. That's
what you always said. (*Raises glass again.*) "Passion and truth,
Sarah . . . that's what we are." (*Pause.*) It isn't true, Philip.
The passion's spent. I can't buy any more. (*Long pause.*) They
say the water's changing. I've seen no porpoises. No seals bark
on the shore. (*Long pause.*) And . . . and . . . the whales
are . . . gone. (*After a long pause, she rises holding her wine
goblet. She turns in place, with an air of resignation and
valediction, and salutes the artifacts of her life in this room.
After one slow revolve, she exits to porch, goes to porch rail
and stares down at the sea. After a brief pause, she raises the
goblet and sips again; and in so doing catches sight of the
moon.*) Oh . . . my . . . (*Ensnared by moonlight for a time
before memory rushes in.*) My corset had so many stays and
so many ties . . . (*Pause.*) You said, "Too many, my love.

54

The moon will set before I have you completely undone." (*A bright laugh of recollection.*) But I said, "Never, my love! I won't be undone entirely, even by you, for what mystery would keep you with me if you unwrapped them all?" (*She turns from the sea, re-enters the living room, dances several waltz steps across to the "anniversary" table, where she again sits and lightly caresses the photograph.*) My Yankee Doodle Dandy . . . (*Now, her hands, as if they were another's, move from the photo to her lap and up her body to caress her face.*) Happy Fourth of July, Philip. Merry Christmas, my love. Happy Birthday, my dear. Will you come to me on St. Valentine's Day? (*Pause.*) Oh, Philip . . . (*Transfixed by present and remembered passions, her hands continue to caress her face and upper body.*) No mademoiselle from Armentiers? Not even one? (*Pause.*) Oh, yes. Ah . . . perfume from Paris! Oh, Philip . . . yes . . . oh, my sweet . . . yes . . . oh . . . (*Her head falls back upon her shoulders and she breathes heavily from her journey of communion and consummation. She recovers her composure; she rises and smiles warmly at the photograph before picking it up; then she moves U. to replace the photo on the mantel. Before she can complete this cross, Libby bursts into the room from her bedroom, dressed in a long, white flannel nightgown, wearing no slippers, no glasses, and with her hair let down.*)

LIBBY. Sarah!!

SARAH. Libby—

LIBBY. Sarah! I couldn't find you! I called and called, but you were gone. I thought you'd run away and hid in a tree so I ran through all the trails 'til finally I came back here. And there you were, perched right on the edge of the rocks below. I was afraid for you. Sarah.

SARAH. I'm all right, Libby.

LIBBY. I tried to call you back to safety. You were almost in his icy reach and you looked so cold, dear.

SARAH. You were dreaming, Libby.

LIBBY. (*Moving to Sarah, reaching for her.*) Sarah, you were

going right to the belly of the whale! I was afraid for you.
SARAH. (*Backing away toward the mantel.*) Libby, please
. . . go back to bed, dear.
LIBBY. Sarah . . . he *is* here.
SARAH. Stop this, Libby.
LIBBY. (*Reaching for Sarah still and managing to grip her shoulder.*) Don't you see?! He's here for both of us!
SARAH. (*Pulling firmly away from Libby and setting Philip's photograph down on the mantel.*) Libby, you can die if you want to. My life is not over! (*Crosses to her bedroom door, opens it, and speaks as she closes the door behind her.*) Good night, Elizabeth Mae. (*Libby stands in place for a long beat, then turns to mantel to "see" what Sarah has placed there. With her hands on Philip's photo, she speaks.*)
LIBBY. (*Very softly.*) Happy Anniversary, Sarah Louise. (*Libby crosses slowly to her platform rocker, and sits, as the lights fade to:*)

BLACK

ACT II

Scene 3

It is early morning, the next day. The lighting is the same as in the play's opening. Waves wash gently upon the shore, gulls cry in morning cacaphony, and the bell buoy rings sporadically.

Libby is discovered sitting in her rocker, just as we left her in the previous scene.

Sarah enters from her bedroom, dressed as in the play's opening. She sees Libby, and silently registers some surprise. She begins clearing the anniversary table, taking everything to the kitchen except the roses, which she places on the mantel next to the photo of Philip, and the candlestick, which she places on the mantel. Libby listens intently as Sarah completes the task. Libby does not speak until Sarah has finished and takes a position facing out the dining area windows.

LIBBY. Sarah Louise . . . ?
SARAH. What, dear?
LIBBY. I don't want to be a bother to you.
SARAH. You're not a bother, dear.
LIBBY. I don't want to be.
SARAH. Of course not, Libby.
LIBBY. It was only a bad dream.
SARAH. That's right.
LIBBY. It was so real.
SARAH. I'm sure it was, Libby.
LIBBY. (*Pause.*) Sarah . . . I won't be leaving in November.
SARAH. No, dear.
LIBBY. We come from strong stock.
SARAH. Yes, we do.
TISHA. (*Off.*) Hal-loo! Hello! Hello! Hello!
SARAH. Coming, Tisha!
TISHA. (*Entering from kitchen, wearing perennial straw hat, yet another bright floral print dress, and carrying binoculars.*) I let m' self in, dear.
SARAH. Good morning, Tisha.
TISHA. Mornin', Sarah. Mornin', Libby.
LIBBY. Good morning, Tisha.
TISHA. Well, I guess I'm a mite early.
SARAH. That's all right, dear.
TISHA. Libby Strong, I haven't seeen your hair down in a

57

dog's age. You should wear it that way more often, dear.

LIBBY. Hmmph.

TISHA. I mean it, dear. It's right attractive. (*Slight pause.*) Well, when's Mr. Maranov due, Sarah?

SARAH. He isn't coming, Tisha.

TISHA. No? (*Sarah nods 'no'.*) Oh, that's too bad, dear.

SARAH. Yes.

LIBBY. (*Slight pause.*) I'll only need my robe then. You don't mind, do you, Tisha?

TISHA. 'Course not, Libby. Y' needn't get all spruced up for me.

SARAH. I'll get it for you, dear.

LIBBY. I'm not an invalid, Sarah. (*Rises.*) I'll get it myself. (*Crosses to bedroom and enters.*)

SARAH. All right, dear.

TISHA. My . . . aren't we the perky one this mornin'?

SARAH. Yes. (*Crosses to "anniversary table" to move it back into place.*)

TISHA. (*Following and speaking softly.*) Is everything all right, Sarah?

SARAH. Yes, Tisha, I hope so.

TISHA. What do y' mean, Sarah?

SARAH. Tisha—

LIBBY. (*Entering wearing robe and slippers, carrying brush, pins and comb.*) We should take some sun.

TISHA. Ayuh, there's nary a speck of breeze.

LIBBY. (*Crossing to porch.*) We won't have many more days like this.

TISHA. That's right, dear. It'd be a shame to miss a minute of it. (*Follows Libby to porch door.*) Comin', Sarah?

SARAH. Yes. (*Libby and Tisha exit to porch; Tisha attempts to assist Libby into her rocker. Sarah lingers inside, then exits to porch after the others.*)

LIBBY. Don't hover, Tisha.

TISHA. 'Course not, dear.

JOSHUA. (*Below.*) Jesus Lord above! (*Sarah crosses U. on porch.*)

LIBBY. Like a bad penny . . .

JOSHUA. (*Below.*) Where's that goddamned wrench?!

LIBBY. I hope the sewer rats ate it, Joshua Brackett!

SARAH. Joshua, you left it in the bathroom!

JOSHUA. (*Below.*) What's that y' say?!

SARAH. I put it in the kitchen!

TISHA. He certainly knows how to raise a ruckus.

LIBBY. The noisiest man God ever created.

JOSHUA. (*Off, in kitchen.*) . . . Mrs. Webber?

SARAH. We're on the porch, Joshua!

LIBBY. Oh, Sarah . . . must you?

SARAH. Yes, dear.

JOSHUA. (*Entering from living room.*) I found it, Mrs. Webber. Mornin', Mrs. Strong . . . Mrs. Doughty.

TISHA. Mornin', Joshua.

LIBBY. Mr. Brackett . .

JOSHUA. Mighty sorry if I disturbed you ladies. Thought I could just sneak in and out without makin' a fuss.

TISHA. That'll be the day, Joshua.

SARAH. Joshua, I've made up my mind about that new window. Do you think you could put it in by Labor Day?

JOSHUA. Well . . . Godfrey Mighty, Mrs. Webber. I'd a' bet you weren't gonna do it.

TISHA. That's the ticket, Sarah!

JOSHUA. I can start tomorrow.

SARAH. Good.

TISHA. Ayuh, be wonderful.

SARAH. It'll be nice to have it for next summer.

JOSHUA. (*Slight pause while he puts his wrench in tool box.*) If y' don't mind my askin', what's got you ladies up so early?

LIBBY. We're waiting for the whales, Mr. Brackett.

JOSHUA. Whales, is it? Well, I expect you'll have a mighty long wait.

LIBBY. The herring are running. That's a sure sign.

JOSHUA. Not any more, it ain't. Nope, don't see 'em in these parts any longer. No sir, they been all fished out. (*Turns to leave on boardwalk.*) Well, ladies, I'll be off. See ya tomorrow, Mrs. Webber. (*Exits on boardwalk.*)

SARAH. All right, Joshua.

LIBBY. Do you see the herring, Tisha?

TISHA. Ayuh . . . there they are . . . out by the channel marker.

LIBBY. Good. We must stay alert for the whales.

SARAH. Libby . . . there haven't been any for two years.

LIBBY. They'll come, right out front, just as they always have.

SARAH. No, Libby.

LIBBY. We'll wait for them together, Sarah.

SARAH. No, Libby. The whales are gone.

TISHA. (*After a pause.*) Well . . . I think I'd better be on my way, girls. (*Pats Libby's hand in farewell.*) Bye, Libby. (*Gives Sarah a kiss.*) Bye, dear.

SARAH. Bye, Tisha.

TISHA. (*Stopping on boardwalk.*) Sarah, if y' need anythin' . . .

SARAH. All right, dear. (*Tisha exits.*)

LIBBY. (*Long pause.*) Sarah . . . you're leaving me, aren't you?

SARAH. (*Pause.*) Yes. I am.

LIBBY. But you're the one who knows my life and all its times.

SARAH. I don't even know my own, Libby.

LIBBY. I don't want our time to be over.

SARAH. It's not over. Just . . . different.

LIBBY. (*Pause.*) Will you have time to brush my hair? (*Raises hairbrush from her lap.*)

SARAH. (*Taking brush.*) Of course, dear. (*Starts brushing.*)

LIBBY. (*Pause.*) What will you do, Sarah?

SARAH. I'm not sure. I may stay on the island this winter.

60

LIBBY. With Tisha?

SARAH. Perhaps.

LIBBY. And hunt for ambergris?

SARAH. I may. It preserves essences, you know.

LIBBY. Yes.

SARAH. (*Pause.*) Libby . . . what will you do?

LIBBY. (*Pause.*) Well . . . I'll ask my Anna to help me find a . . . companion in Philadelphia. (*Pause.*) Anna will do that for me, Sarah.

SARAH. Yes, of course she will.

LIBBY. (*Pause.*) Life fooled me. (*Pause.*) Always does. (*Long pause.*) Is my hair as white as the swans?

SARAH. I expect it is.

LIBBY. You're not fibbing?

SARAH. No, dear.

LIBBY. Not yellowing at all?

SARAH. No, dear.

LIBBY. I've always had beautiful hair.

SARAH. Yes, you have.

LIBBY. (*After a long pause.*) I love you, Sarah Louise. (*She raises a hand toward Sarah.*)

SARAH. (*Long pause.*) And I love you, Elizabeth Mae. (*Sarah comes to Libby's side, puts down the brush, and takes Libby's hand in both of hers. Libby begins to rock very slightly. The sisters continue to hold hands as a lone gull flies overhead from L. to R., from bay to open sea, crying as it flies. They follow its flight with sighted and sightless eyes as the lights fade to:*)

CURTAIN

THE END

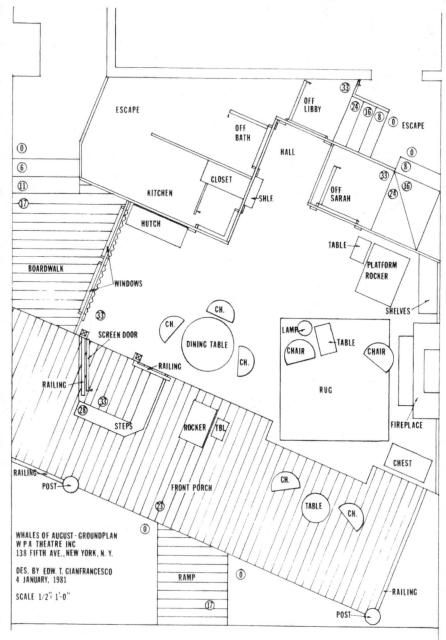

ESCAPE

OFF LIBBY

OFF BATH

HALL

③③ ㉔ ⑯ ⑧ ⓪ ESCAPE

⓪
⑥
⑪
⑰

⓪
③③ ⑧
⑯
㉔

CLOSET

KITCHEN

SHLF.

OFF SARAH

HUTCH

TABLE

BOARDWALK

WINDOWS

PLATFORM ROCKER

SHELVES

③③

CH.

CH.

DINING TABLE

CH.

LAMP

TABLE

CHAIR

CHAIR

SCREEN DOOR

RAILING

RAILING

RUG

FIREPLACE

㉘ ③③

STEPS

ROCKER TBL

CHEST

RAILING

POST

FRONT PORCH

CH.

TABLE

CH.

㉓

⓪

RAILING

WHALES OF AUGUST - GROUNDPLAN
W P A THEATRE INC
138 FIFTH AVE., NEW YORK, N.Y.

DES. BY EDW. T. GIANFRANCESCO
4 JANUARY, 1981

SCALE 1/2"= 1'-0"

RAMP

⓪

POST

⑰

62

PROPERTY PLOT

ACT ONE

Scene 1:

Wicker laundry basket containing dish towels, one red and
one white rose
Handkerchief for Sarah
In kitchen closet, feather duster (or dust cloth)
On mantel, photograph of Philip
On mantel, silver candlestick
On mantel, at least one brass knickknack
On Libby's side table, breakfast tray with cereal bowl, tea cup
and saucer
In kitchen, tall white taper
In Libby's bedroom, Libby's shoes, brush, comb, hairpins,
and brooch
In living room, "tourist" sombrero

Scene 2:

Sewing basket, needle and thread, and apron for Sarah
Small berry pail containing a few berries for Tisha
In kitchen, tea tray with tea pot, 3 cups, 3 saucers, creamer,
sugar bowl, and 3 spoons
Wooden tool box for Joshua
Bamboo fishing pole for Maranov
Burlap bag with unseen fish for Maranov
In Libby's bedroom, Libby's glasses (dark)

Scene 3:

On dining table, Sarah's sewing basket and apron
In kitchen, three place settings of china and silverware
In kitchen, three napkins in silver napkin rings
In kitchen, three water goblets

ACT TWO

Scene 1:

On dining table, three dinner plates, three water goblets, and three settings of silverware
In kitchen, coffee tray with coffee pot, 3 cups, 3 saucers, sugar bowl, creamer, and 3 spoons
Emerald ring wrapped in handkerchief for Maranov

Scene 2:

In dining area cupboard drawer, linen tablecloth
On dining area cupboard, cut glass wine decanter containing red wine.
On dining area cupboard, one cut glass wine goblet
On mantel, candlestick with white taper
On mantel, boxed wooden matches
On mantel, photograph of Philip
In kitchen, slender cut glass vase containing one red and one white rose

Scene 3:

On "anniversary" table, linen tablecloth
On "anniversary" table, candlestick and taper
On "anniversary" table, cut glass vase with roses
On "anniversary" table, boxed wooden matches
Binoculars for Tisha
In Libby's bedroom, Libby's slippers, robe, brush, comb, and hairpins
Wooden tool box for Joshua
Pipe wrench for Joshua